CHE

Favourite Courses

Published with the support
and encouragement of

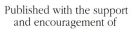 

Published by
Motivate Publishing

Dubai: PO Box 2331, Dubai, UAE
Tel: (04) 824060 Fax: (04) 824436

Abu Dhabi: PO Box 43072, Abu Dhabi, UAE
Tel: (02) 271666 Fax: (02) 271888

London: Macmillan House, 96 Kensington High Street,
London W8 4SG
Tel: (0171) 9377733 Fax: (0171) 9377293

Directors:
Obaid Humaid Al Tayer
Ian Fairservice

Publishing Manager: *Catherine Demangeot*
Editor: *Kate John*
Art Director: *Roy Thomas*
Photographer: *Adiseshan Shankar*

First published 1996

© 1996 François Porté
and Motivate Publishing

ISBN 1 86063 023 5

British Library Cataloguing-in-Publication Data.
A catalogue record for this book is available from
the British Library.

Printed by Rashid Printers, Ajman

Since arriving in Dubai I have been amazed by the variety of fresh ingredients available in Dubai. Also, over the years I have witnessed a plethora of international restaurants opening in the Gulf region and with them comes the introduction of different cultures and their specialist cuisine. Being largely self-taught, I have taken up the exciting opportunity to try a fresh approach to many of the classic dishes accumulated in my culinary repertoire. This book bears witness to just some of the delicious influences of the Gulf and all the ingredients it has on offer.

Impressed by other cuisines, from Arabic to Italian, I have come to regard their ingredients as basic essentials in my own kitchen: olive oil, balsamic vinegar, couscous, spices and fresh herbs, all of which feature in this cookbook. Fresh produce can be purchased daily and there is a wealth of choice in the specialist food souks.

As a seasoned chef, the best advice I can impart to cooks of all abilities is: develop your own creative flair for the food you are preparing – from flavour and food combinations, to presentation. This book comprises a selection of my personal favourites, also popular with regular diners of 'Le Classique' restaurant at the Emirates Golf Club. As the photographs show, I am always careful to present food in its most natural state, in terms of flavour, texture and colour; it is crucial not to overpower these important, and often delicate, elements.

One of the best ways to overcome the problem of conflicting flavours is to be in charge of the ingredients, right down to the stock and sauce you use. Convenience foods may save time but should be used in moderation. Homemade stocks lend a superb flavour, and can be made from leftover bones, poultry carcasses and vegetables. Many butchers will supply these, whilst the fish market is a good source for fish bones. A selection of basic homemade sauces and sundries accompany dishes throughout this book; while they may initially daunt the cook, after the first few attempts, they will become second nature to make.

The famous *mise en place* is a cook's best asset, as the total preparation time may be more than half accounted for – from making stocks and sauces, to peeling vegetables and filleting fish – in advance. Wherever appropriate, I have highlighted cooking and preparation 'tips' with the recipes, which aim to simplify many tasks, and offer alternatives to selective ingredients.

I will have realised my purpose if this book helps you conjure new and enticing recipes at home and indulge in the tastes of the Gulf.

François Porté

Conversion Tables

Weights

Metric	Imperial	N. American
10 g	$^{1}/_{2}$ oz	$^{1}/_{2}$ oz
20 g	$^{3}/_{4}$ oz	$^{3}/_{4}$ oz
25 g	1 oz	1 oz
50 g	2 oz	$^{1}/_{4}$ cup
75 g	3 oz	3 oz
125 g	4 oz	$^{1}/_{2}$ cup
150 g	5 oz	5 oz
175 g	6 oz	$^{3}/_{4}$ cup
200 g	7 oz	7 oz
250 g	9 oz	9 oz
300 g	11 oz	11 oz
400 g	14 oz	$1^{3}/_{4}$ cup
450 g	16 oz (1 lb)	2 cups
700 g	$1^{1}/_{2}$ lbs	3 cups
900 g	2 lbs	4 cups
1.1 kg	$2^{1}/_{2}$ lbs	$2^{1}/_{2}$ lbs
1.4 kg	3 lbs	3 lbs
2 kg	$4^{1}/_{2}$ lbs	$4^{1}/_{2}$ lbs

Liquid capacity

Metric	Imperial	N. American
25 ml	1 fl oz	1 fl oz
50 ml	2 fl oz	$^{1}/_{3}$ cup
75 ml	3 fl oz	3 fl oz
125 ml	4 fl oz	$^{1}/_{2}$ cup
150 ml	5 fl oz ($^{1}/_{4}$ pt)	$^{2}/_{3}$ cup
200 ml	7 fl oz	7 fl oz
300 ml	10 fl oz ($^{1}/_{2}$ pt)	$1^{1}/_{3}$ cup
600 ml	20 fl oz (1 pt)	2 cups
725 ml	$1^{1}/_{4}$ pts	$1^{1}/_{4}$ pts
1 litre	$1^{3}/_{4}$ pts	$1^{3}/_{4}$ pts

Oven temperatures

°F	°C	GAS MARK
250	130	$^{1}/_{2}$
275	140	1
300	150	2
325	170	3
350	180	4
375	190	5
400	200	6
425	220	7
450	230	8
475	240	9

Abbreviations

tbsp — tablespoon
tsp — teaspoon
g — gramme
kg — kilogramme
ml — millilitre
pt — pint

The tableware and accessories featured in the food photography were supplied by IKEA and Emirates Golf Club.

The Recipes

Starters

Fish Dishes

Meat Dishes

Desserts

Sauces and Sundries

❝One of the great joys of my profession is the endless discovery of authentic international cuisines – and with that discovery comes the wonderful opportunity to sample an array of exotic spices and herbs – each of which can either transform a dish or, at the very least, enhance it with a uniquely subtle flavour.**❞**

The Recipes

Cigali Salad with Smoked Trout
dill mayonnaise

4 fresh cigalis,
  shells on
320 g smoked sea
  trout fillets
1 avocado, peeled
  and sliced
1 mango, peeled
  and diced
2 hard-boiled eggs
  cut into 12
  wedges
8 tbsps
  mayonnaise,
  (see p 88)
6 tbsps vinaigrette,
  (see p 87)
6 red cherry
  tomatoes,
  quartered
a few peas
2 tbsps chopped
  dill
mixed salad
  leaves

Preparation time:
30 minutes
Cooking time:
10 minutes
Serves 4

1. Cook the cigalis in boiling water for about 10 minutes. Strain.

2. Remove the meat from the shells and cut up into 3 equal pieces, lengthwise.

3. Divide the smoked trout into 12 equal portions.

4. To serve, mix together the mayonnaise and dill. Place 2 tbsps in the centre of each plate. Surround the mayonnaise alternately with the cigalis, smoked trout, avocado, eggs, sliced mango, cherry tomatoes and peas.

5. Toss the salad leaves with 3 tbsps of vinaigrette and place a handful in the centre of each plate. Spoon the rest of the dressing around the edge of each plate.

Chef's tip: Cigalis are in season from November to February. Do not be tempted to use frozen cigalis for this dish, they are no substitute for the fresh ingredient, which may be bought at the fish market.

66 *This stunning fish salad is my absolute favourite dish to make. Your guests will be enormously impressed by the choice of refreshing ingredients. An alternative to cigalis is lobster, while smoked mackerel may be used instead of smoked trout, and papaya is as mouth-watering as mango.* 99

Baked Field Mushrooms with Snails
garlic and parsley crust

*12 large field
mushrooms
36 snails, tinned
3 cloves garlic
160 g fresh white
breadcrumbs
1 onion, chopped
160 ml white wine
200 g butter, room
temperature
a pinch of cayenne
pepper
4 tsps flat-leaf
parsley
salt and pepper*

*Preparation time:
20 minutes
Cooking time:
20 minutes
Serves 4*

1. Heat the oven to 375°F/190°C/Gas Mark 5. Wipe the mushrooms and remove the stalks setting them aside.

2. Sweat the onion with 80 g of the butter until softened. Then add the chopped mushroom stalks and continue cooking for a few minutes before adding the white wine. Cook until all the liquid has evaporated. Put aside to cool.

3. To prevent the mushroom cups shrinking too much, pre-cook them before stuffing with the filling. Brush each cup with a little olive oil in an ovenproof dish and bake in the oven for 5 to 6 minutes. Keep the juices aside after cooking.

4. Place the parsley, garlic and cooled mushroom mixture, cayenne and seasoning in a food processor and blend to a paste-like consistency.

5. Transfer to a bowl and add the remaining soft butter and breadcrumbs, mix well.

6. Fill each mushroom cup with 3 snails and mould the mushroom mixture lightly into a dome shape, covering the snails.

7. Place the mushrooms in an ovenproof dish, adding the mushroom juices to the bottom of the dish and bake for 12 to 15 minutes.

Chef's tip: The mushrooms should be very fresh and white in colour and it is important they are cup shaped, to hold the filling. Field mushrooms also shrink a good deal during cooking.

66 *A rich and substantial dish, with the succulent filling of buttery snails in garlic – a taste sensation and a tempting variation of the popular baked mushroom starter.* 99

Fresh Asparagus with Smoked Salmon
lemon butter sauce and caviar

24 green asparagus
140 g smoked
** salmon**
80 g Sevruga caviar
180 ml butter sauce,
** (see p 89)**
juice of 1 lemon
$\frac{1}{2}$ tomato, diced
a sprig of fresh dill

Preparation time:
30 minutes
Cooking time:
10 minutes
Serves 4

1. Peel asparagus, trim the woody ends and cook in boiling salted water for 8 to 10 minutes. Drain and refresh in ice water. Strain and dry.

2. Slice the salmon as thinly as possible using a sharp knife. You will need 3 slices for each plate.

3. Form the salmon into rosettes and keep chilled.

4. Add the lemon juice to the warmed butter sauce.

5. To serve, warm the asparagus for a few seconds in hot water, place 2 tbsps of lemon butter sauce on the serving plate, and arrange the asparagus on top.

6. Scoop the caviar and place it on one side of the asparagus and the salmon rosette on the other side. Garnish with finely diced tomato and a sprig of fresh dill.

Chef's tip: Pre-sliced smoked salmon is available in local supermarkets.

❝A superb combination of salmon and caviar with a tangy lemon butter sauce; the flavours of this dish are distinct yet delicate, while the sophisticated presentation will naturally impress the most discerning diner.❞

Salad of Monkfish, Red Mullet, and Mussels
saffron and tomato butter vinaigrette

4 small red
   mullets, cleaned
   and filleted
200 g monkfish
   fillet, sliced into
   12 pieces
12 large mussels
80 ml white wine
40 ml clarified
   butter
2 tbsps red wine
   vinegar
2 tbsps tomato
   coulis (see p 87)
2 tbsps tomato juice
4 tbsps tapenade,
   (see p 93)
60 ml fish stock,
   (see p 86)
40 ml olive oil
a pinch of saffron
a selection of mixed
   salad leaves,
   tossed with 2 tbsps
   basic vinaigrette
   (see p 87)

Preparation time:
20 minutes
Cooking time:
15 minutes
Serves 4

For the sauce
1. Reduce the vinegar and white wine until 1 tbsp is left in the pan.
2. Add the fish stock, bring to boil and reduce to 60 ml.
3. Add the tomato coulis with tomato juice and tarragon. Then add the clarified butter. Season with salt and pepper. Set aside.

Cooking the fish
Heat the oil until smoking in a pan, toss in the red mullet fillets and fry over high heat for 1 minute on both sides. Repeat with the monkfish and the mussels.

To serve, place the fish alternately around the border of each plate. Add the tapenade on top of the red mullet and pour the sauce on top of the fish to form a pool on the plate. To finish, place a handful of salad in the middle of each plate. Serve immediately.

Chef's tip: Red mullet's soft texture contrasts well here with the firmer flesh of the monkfish. Variations of fish for this dish are seabream with hammour and lobster.

Simply, a seafood symphony with strong Mediterranean flavours.

Pumpkin Soup with Lemon Grass
coconut cream

Approx. 2 kg
 pumpkin
1.5 litres chicken
 stock (see p 86)
2 onions, chopped
2 stalks lemon
 grass, chopped
8 lemon leaves,
 shredded
2 tomatoes,
 chopped
$^1/_2$ tsp turmeric
1 green chilli,
 seedless and
 chopped
6 tbsps cream
 coconut, tinned
30 g butter
10 ml olive oil
60 ml whipped
 cream
a few coriander
 leaves
salt and pepper

Preparation time:
30 minutes
Cooking time:
30 minutes
Serves 6 to 8

1. Pre-heat the oven to 400°F/200°C/Gas Mark 6. Cut the pumpkin in half and scoop out the seeds and stringy fibres. Keep the bottom half aside if you wish, in which to serve the soup. Peel the upper half, cut the pumpkin into cubes and place in a saucepan. Use just enough chicken stock to cover the pumpkin and cook over a medium heat for about 20 minutes until tender.

2. Place the bottom half of the pumpkin on a baking sheet, brush the outside with olive oil and bake in an oven for 30 minutes until the flesh is half-cooked. Set aside.

3. Put the chopped onion, lemon grass, chilli and lemon leaves in a separate saucepan with the butter and cook for 3 to 4 minutes until the onion is transparent. Add the turmeric, tomatoes, coconut milk and remaining chicken stock. Cook for 20 minutes to allow the flavours to develop.

4. Purée the cooked pumpkin in a food processor and transfer to the saucepan.

5. Blend the onion mixture in an electric blender and sieve before adding to the pumpkin purée.

6. Add the chicken stock or water as necessary to adjust the consistency. Bring the soup to the boil and simmer for 2 to 3 minutes. Adjust the seasoning.

7. Serve the soup in warmed soup bowls or in the baked pumpkin shell. Garnish with 1 tbsp whipped cream and chopped coriander leaves.

Chef's tip: This soup may instead be prepared using vegetable stock (see p 86) to suit vegetarians. Serving it chilled is another option.

A deliciously smooth, wholesome soup with an oriental gesture of lemon grass and coconut.

Beef Carpaccio with Ratatouille
honey and peppercorn dressing

260 g fresh fillet of beef, in one piece
180 g ratatouille (see p 87)
4 artichoke bottoms, fresh or tinned
36 green peppercorns
80 g finely grated Parmesan cheese
8 pastry sticks, made with puff pastry
1 tsp honey
1 tsp balsamic vinegar
140 ml basic vinaigrette (see p 87)
1 tbsp fried leek

Preparation time:
20 minutes
Cooking time:
6 minutes
Serves 4

1. Chill the beef fillet in the freezer until firm before slicing thinly, preferably using a meat slicer. Alternatively, use a sharp knife to cut slices, allowing 65 g per person then place the slices between two layers of clingfilm and flatten with a rolling pin.

2. Blend the peppercorns, honey and the balsamic vinegar with the basic vinaigrette.

3. Mix the ratatouille with 2 tbsps of the dressing.

Pastry Sticks

On a lightly floured surface, roll out $1/2$ pack of puff pastry to $1/2$cm thick rectangle. Divide into 8 strips and roll each one into thin cigar shapes, giving them a little twist. Brush with egg wash and then roll in grated Parmesan cheese. Cook in a pre-heated oven, 400°F/200°C/Gas Mark 6 for 5 to 6 minutes. Remove from oven and place on a wire tray to cool. Cut as desired as a garnish.

To serve, lay the beef slices neatly on the plates, arrange an artichoke filled with a spoonful of ratatouille in the centre of the plate. On top of this, place two pastry sticks and arrange the Parmesan cheese around the edges of the plate. Brush generously with the dressing.

Chef's tip: There is no substitute for using fresh beef; ask the butcher to trim off any excess fat. If the dish is going to be prepared in advance, flatten the carpaccio with clingfilm to retain the colour.

❝Balsamic vinegar added to vinaigrette imparts a rich and distinctive flavour to the dressing used in this recipe. Fine strips of leek, lightly fried in olive oil, add an unusual touch to the final presentation and a crisp bite to the dish.❞

Tartare of Salmon and Cigali
tabbouleh salad

200 g fresh salmon fillet
2 fresh cigalis, cooked
    for 2 minutes
40 g courgette, finely
    diced and blanched
40 g yellow pepper,
    finely diced and
    blanched
20 baby tomatoes
juice of 1 lime
a pinch of coriander

FOR THE TABBOULEH
80 g bulgur, soaked for
    20 minutes
6 tbsps flat-leaf parsley,
    chopped
3 tbsps mint leaves,
    chopped
120 g tomato, diced
80 g red onion, chopped
1 clove garlic,
    chopped
juice of $\frac{1}{2}$ lemon
3 tbsps olive oil

DRESSING
segment of 1 lemon
120 ml olive oil
60 ml basic vinaigrette
    (see p 87)

Preparation time:
35 minutes
Serves 4

Tartare
1. Peel the cigalis and cut them diagonally into fine strips and place in a bowl.
2. Marinate with lime juice, salt and coriander powder, cover and place in the refrigerator for 2 hours.
3. Slice the salmon paper thin and marinate as above.

Tabbouleh and dressing
Combine all the ingredients for the tabbouleh. Season and refrigerate. Prepare the dressing by combining all the ingredients.

To assemble
Finely chop the marinated salmon and cigali. Transfer to a bowl and add the courgettes and yellow peppers. Mix gently and season to taste.

To serve, pack the terrine firmly into a little china Arabic cup and turn out in the middle of a serving plate. Arrange 5 tsps of tabbouleh around the tartare alternating with the baby tomatoes. Spoon the dressing around the plate and decorate as desired.

Chef's tip: When out of season, cigalis can be substituted for prawns which are always readily available. Gravalax or marinated salmon can be bought at larger Gulf supermarkets.

66 *Well-known in the Middle East, tabbouleh is used in this recipe as a background for the salmon and cigalis, both for its rich tapestry of colour and its distinctive flavour.* 99

Mushroom and Ricotta Tortellini
tomato coulis and olive salsa

250 g assorted
field and wild
  mushrooms,
  chopped
40 g butter
1 onion, chopped
1 clove garlic
60 ml white wine
80 g cooked
  spinach
60 g grated
  Parmesan
120 ml tomato
  coulis (see p 87)
  with ½ tsp basil
180 g fresh pasta,
  (see p 90)
45 g tapenade,
  (see p 93)
80 g ricotta cheese
120 ml cream
20 small fresh
  basil leaves,
  gently fried in oil
pastry sticks,
  (see p 18)

Preparation time:
30 minutes
Cooking time:
6 minutes
Serves 4

1. Sweat the onion for 1 minute in a saucepan with 40 g of butter. Add the mushrooms, garlic and continue cooking until softened.

2. Add the white wine and cook until all the liquid has evaporated. Then add the spinach, season with salt and pepper.

3. Transfer to a chopping board and chop finely, then place in a bowl and mix in the ricotta cheese.

4. Roll the pasta dough out as thinly as possible on a floured surface. Cut into rounds using a 6-cm cutter. Place 1 tsp of filling in the centre of each round. Brush the rounds with water and fold in half sealing the rounds carefully. Shape into tortellini.

5. Cook the tortellini in boiling, salted water for 2 to 3 minutes only. Remove and drain.

6. Place the cream in a saucepan with 30 g Parmesan and seasoning. Bring to the boil for 1 minute or until the sauce has thickened slightly.

To serve, arrange the tortellini in an ovenproof serving dish and pour the cream over. Place 1 tbsp of tomato coulis in the middle of the dish and add a little of the tapenade on top of each tortellini. Sprinkle with remaining Parmesan and place under the grill for 30 seconds before serving. Decorate each serving with basil leaves and pastry sticks.

Chef's tip: Alternative fillings for the tortellini include pine nuts and spinach.

“Fresh pasta is impossible to surpass on the taste front, especially in the case of this mouth-watering combination. The simplest way to make it successfully is by using a pasta machine.”

Prawn Butterfly with Crab Salad
spicy citrus vinaigrette

SPICY DRESSING
1 orange
1 tsp honey
30 ml white wine
vinegar
80 ml sunflower
oil

12 fresh tiger
prawns
2 soft-boiled eggs
40 g Sevruga
caviar
1 small cucumber
80 g French beans
16 orange
segments
2 tomatoes,
skinned and cut
into segments
a few chives

CRAB SALAD
160 g fresh
blue crab
1 tbsp chopped
onion
2 tbsps skinned
tomatoes, diced
1 tbsp diced
red pepper
juice of ½ lemon
1 tbsp mayonnaise
2 tsps chives,
chopped

Preparation time:
35 minutes
Serves 4

Spicy dressing
This may be prepared in advance and set aside. Whisk together in a blender zest and juice of the orange and add all the other dressing ingredients. Add to this, 1 tsp turmeric, 1 tsp mild curry paste and a pinch of mixed spice.

Prawns and crab salad
1. Pass wooden skewers through the middle of the prawns.
2. Cook the prawns in boiling vegetable water for 2 to 3 minutes. Refresh in cold water and remove from the skewers. Peel carefully.
3. Make an incision along the back of the prawn to remove the gritty vein that runs down its length.
4. Marinate the prawns with spicy dressing and refrigerate for 24 hours.
5. Cook the live crab in a covered saucepan of boiling water for 5 to 6 minutes, or a little longer if the crab is rather big. Strain and cool. Tinned crabmeat may be used as an alternative.
6. Mix the crab and all the ingredients in a bowl.

To serve, place one large tablespoon of the crab salad in the centre of each plate, and arrange 3 prawns on top. Decorate with remaining ingredients as illustrated and drizzle each plate with dressing.

Chef's tip: The skewers help prevent the prawns curling during cooking.

"This starter will delight anyone who enjoys the refreshing blend of shellfish and citrus with the added luxury of caviar, all presented in a visually tempting design, while for the cook, this is a wonderfully simple dish to create."

Cabbage with Prawn Mousseline
ginger and coriander sauce

1 savoy cabbage

PRAWN MOUSSE
220 g cleaned
  prawns, chilled
3 egg whites
180 ml cream
a pinch of cayenne
  pepper
salt

THE SAUCE
80 ml white wine
280 ml vegetable
  stock (see p 86)
½ tsp freshly
  chopped ginger
60 ml cream
100 g butter
½ tsp lemon juice
1 tbsp coriander,
  chopped

Preparation time:
35 minutes
Cooking time:
6 minutes
Serves 4

1. Cut the chilled prawns into cubes.

2. Place in a food processor with the egg whites, cayenne pepper and salt to taste. Process to smooth paste and add the cream slowly until blended but do not over process. You should end up with a mousse-like texture. If preferred, push through a fine sieve for a smoother mousse.

Coriander and ginger sauce

In a saucepan, reduce the white wine by half. Add the vegetable stock and the freshly chopped ginger. Continue cooking until reduced by approx. 80 ml. Now add the cream and cook for 1 minute. Then whisk in the butter and chopped coriander. Check the seasoning.

To assemble

1. Blanch 4 savoy cabbage leaves in salted water for 2 to 3 minutes. Refresh in ice water and drain well.

2. Spread the cabbage leaves on a flat surface and place 2 to 3 tbsps of prawn mixture in the centre of each one. Roll up to form a ball shape, tucking the edges of the leaves underneath.

3. Steam the cabbages for 5 to 6 minutes depending on the size.

Chef's tip: The illustration shows the parcels decorated with small Chinese mushrooms and brunoise of vegetables.

66 *The pleasant surprise of creamy mousse beneath the vivid green cabbage will certainly impress any guest, while the fresh ginger adds a hint of exotic cuisine.* 99

Red Pepper Gateau with Lentil Salad

FOR THE ROULADE
400 g red pepper,
 chopped
8 eggs, separated

LENTIL SALAD
150 g green lentils
1 stalk celery, finely
 chopped
1/2 red onion,
 finely chopped
60 g cucumber,
 finely chopped
60 g carrot, finely
 chopped and cooked
juice of 1/2 lemon
2 tbsp mayonnaise,
 (see p 88)
1 tsp soy sauce

TO GARNISH
1 avocado
1 tomato, diced
100 g feta cheese,
 cut into triangles
40 ml basic vinaigrette
 (see p 87)
4 strips of leek,
 blanched
1 cooked beetroot

Preparation time:
40 minutes
Cooking time:
40 minutes
Serves 4

1. Grease and line a 10 x 12in Swiss roll tin with greaseproof paper. Heat the oven to 350°F/180°C/ Gas Mark 4.
2. Cook the chopped red pepper in boiling water until tender. Drain well. Put in a blender and liquidise.
3. Sieve into a bowl and add the egg yolks and seasoning.
4. Whisk 6 of the egg whites until stiff and fold lightly into the red pepper. Season with salt and pepper.
5. Turn into the prepared tin and level.
6. Bake for 8 to 10 minutes or until the top is dry and springy to the touch.

Lentil salad

Simmer the lentils in a saucepan until tender, approx. 30 minutes. Drain and cool. Transfer to a bowl and add the rest of the ingredients. Mix well and adjust the seasoning.

To assemble

1. Line the inside of a 7in pastry cutter with strips of the red pepper roulade.
2. Fill with the lentil salad packing it down firmly.
3. Spread the chopped tomato evenly over the top and remove the pastry cutter very gently.
4. Place a leek strip around each gateau, tie a knot and place it in the middle of each plate.
5. Surround the gateau with the sliced beetroot arranged in a ring on the plate.
6. Peel and slice the avocado and arrange around the outside of the beetroot ring with the feta cheese fanned out in a star shape. Spoon the dressing around the plate.

66 *A vegetarian delight with a bouquet of colour and contrasting flavours – the sweetness of the red pepper complements the sharp, savoury cheese. As a variation of ingredients, a spinach or broccoli roulade is equally delicious.* 99

Chicken and Duck Terrine
two sauces

400 g boned and
 skinless chicken
 breast
1 x 180 g tin foie
 gras, diced
160 g smoked duck
 breast, thinly
 sliced lengthwise
 (preferably in a
 meat slicer)
450 g chicken
 stock (see p 86)
180 ml whipping
 cream
1 large carrot,
 cooked and diced
180 g unsalted
 butter
freshly ground
 pepper
a pinch of cayenne
 pepper
18 tbsps cocktail
 sauce (see p 88)

CHEESE SAUCE
10 tbsps full-fat
 soft cheese
 blended with
 2 tbsps cream

Preparation time:
50 minutes
Cooking time:
15 minutes
Serves 10 to 12

1. Place the chicken breast in a saucepan with the stock. Bring to boil, cover and simmer very gently for 8 to 10 minutes or until the chicken is just cooked. Remove from the liquid and set aside, covered.

2. Bring the stock to a rapid boil and reduce to approx. 8 to 10 tbsps.

3. Add the cream, and reduce once more by about half.

4. When the chicken and stock have cooled down, transfer to a food processor and blend until smooth. Add the butter to the mixture and blend thoroughly for 30 seconds.

5. Transfer to a bowl. Fold in the carrot and foie gras. Season to taste with salt and freshly ground black pepper and a pinch of cayenne pepper.

6. It is recommended to slice the smoked duck breast whilst still frozen, as it retains its shape better in the meat slicer.

To assemble

Line a 2pt loaf tin smoothly with clingfilm overhanging the edges. Arrange the smoked duck strips over base and vertical sides of the tin so that the duck hangs over the edges. Now fill the tin with the chicken mixture so that it comes to the very top. Fold the duck strips over and patch any gaps then fold over the clingfilm. Chill overnight.

To serve, turn out the terrine and cut into 1½cm thick slices using a knife that has been heated in boiling water. It is best to serve the terrine at room temperature, to enable each slice to 'relax' and to enhance the smooth texture. Lay each slice on a large plate and alternate the prepared cocktail and cheese sauces along one side of the terrine slice. Garnish with a jardiniere of vegetables or salad leaves.

“A marvellous terrine that can be easily prepared in advance.
Its subtle combination of flavours are further heightened by the
smoked duck border and colourful contrast of sauces. While this
is a visually captivating dish, due to its delicate assembly it is less
suitable for large functions, such as buffets. ”

Sultan Ibrahim with Ginger Noodles
vinaigrette marinière

4 to 6 red mullets,
   scaled and filleted
160 g Chinese noodles
½ tsp chopped
   ginger
a few drops of
   soy sauce
4 sheets of seaweed,
   finely shredded
40 ml olive oil

MARINIERE
1 tbsp carrot
1 tbsp courgette
1 tbsp red pepper
1 tbsp yellow pepper
1 tbsp fennel
2 tomatoes, skinned
   and diced
1 tbsp wild rice,
   cooked
1 tsp each of chives,
   parsley, basil,
   tarragon.
160 ml fish stock,
   (see p 86)
a pinch of saffron
80 ml olive oil
1 tsp tarragon vinegar
1 tsp balsamic vinegar

Preparation time:
20 minutes
Cooking time:
20 minutes
Serves 4

Marinière
1. Boil the wild rice. Drain.
2. Chop all the vegetables very finely. Cook them in fish stock with saffron for 30 seconds and strain through a sieve. Reduce the fish stock to 80 ml.
3. Place all the ingredients in a bowl and add the olive oil, the balsamic and tarragon vinegar, the reduced fish stock, salt and pepper and set aside to infuse.
4. Stir-fry the Chinese noodles with ginger and soy sauce.
5. Pan-fry the red mullet fillets in the hot olive oil, skin side for 3 minutes and 2 minutes on the other.
6. Deep-fry the shredded seaweed until crispy.

To serve, place the ginger noodles in the centre of each plate. Arrange 2 or 3 fish fillets on the noodles. Pour the sauce around and garnish with the seaweed.

Chef's tip: Seaweed is available at the specialist oriental counters found in many Gulf supermarkets.

*This attractive oriental dish may equally be served as a starter, using smaller red mullets.*

Salmon with Caviar
butter sauce

720 g fresh
salmon fillet,
skinned and
boned
40 g Sevruga
caviar
40 g salmon roe
180 ml butter
sauce, (see p 89)
160 ml champagne
80 g carrot, peeled
80 g courgette
16 baby
asparagus tips
40 g mangetout
40 g celery
salt and pepper
4 baby tomatoes
16 stalks of chives

Preparation time:
20 minutes
Cooking time:
8 minutes
Serves 4

1. Pre-heat the oven to 400°F/200°C/Gas Mark 6. Check the salmon for any remaining pin bones. This can be done by running the flat of the fingers over the fish against the grain. If bones are detected remove them with tweezers. Then cut the fillet into 4 equal portions.

2. Cut the vegetables into fine slices lengthwise, and the slices into matchsticks. Blanch in boiling water for 2 to 3 minutes. Refresh in iced water and drain.

3. Place the salmon steaks in an ovenproof dish with the champagne. Cover with greaseproof paper and bake in the oven for approx. 8 minutes.

4. Remove from the oven and carefully lift out the fish. Keep warm.

5. Pour the juices into a saucepan and reduce to 3 tbsps. Then add the butter sauce with the caviar and salmon roe and warm the sauce through but do not allow it to boil.

To serve, heat the vegetables and place a portion in the centre of each serving plate. Arrange the salmon on top of these and pour the sauce around the plate. Garnish with tomatoes and chives.

Chef's tip: Keep a careful watch on the salmon as it is important not to let it overcook.

66 *The culinary delicacy of caviar crowns the salmon with a rich, exotic sauce.* 99

Pan-fried Fillets of Seabream 'Provençale'
tomato jus and olive salsa

8 fillets of seabream,
  cleaned and scaled
4 tsps pesto
  (see p 88)
320 ml tomato
  sauce (see p 91)
80 ml vegetable stock,
  (see p 86)
1 small fennel, cut
  into 8 lengthwise
½ small courgette,
  cut into 8 lengthwise
1 red pepper,
  skinned, cut into 4
2 tomatoes, skinned,
  cut into 8 segments
4 cooked asparagus
  tips
2 artichoke hearts,
  cut into 8, fresh or
  tinned
1 clove garlic,
  chopped
20 black olives
30 ml olive oil
½ tsp thyme,
  chopped
1 handful deep-fried
  flat-leaf parsley

Preparation time:
20 minutes
Cooking time:
15 minutes
Serves 4

For the tomato jus
Heat the tomato sauce and add vegetable stock. Cook for 5 minutes and pass through a fine sieve. Season to taste.

1. Arrange all the vegetables on a baking tray and sprinkle with thyme and garlic. Drizzle the olive oil on top. Bake in the oven for approx. 10 to 12 minutes.
2. Season the fish fillets and pan-fry in olive oil for 3 minutes each.
3. To serve, arrange a portion of vegetables on the centre of each plate and place a fillet on top. Place more vegetables on the fish fillet and then top with a second piece of fish. Sprinkle with fried parsley.
4. Pour the sauce around the plate and drizzle a few drops of pesto with the olives.

Chef's tip: Seabream may be replaced with salmon if preferred, though the salmon has a more delicate flesh and should be handled carefully once pan-fried.

66 *A delicious reminder of my home in the South of France;
a firm favourite and a stylish dish that is always
best eaten alfresco.* 99

Pan-roasted Fillet of Mérou
basil beurre blanc with diced tomatoes

**4 x 200 g fillets
 of hammour
2 tomatoes,
 skinned, seeded
 and diced
2 tbsps chopped
 basil
260 ml beurre
 blanc, (see p 89)
1 tsp lemon juice
30 ml olive oil
20 g butter
salt and pepper**

*Preparation time:
15 minutes
Cooking time:
10 minutes
Serves 4*

1. Pre-heat the oven to 400°F/200°C/Gas Mark 6. Season the hammour fillets.

2. Heat the butter and olive oil in a frying pan and cook the fish fillets for 2 minutes on each side. Transfer to an ovenproof dish and cook in the oven for approx. 8 minutes.

3. Add the tomatoes, basil and lemon juice to the hot butter sauce but do not boil.

4. Arrange the fish fillets on one half of each plate and place a selection of vegetables on the other half. Pour the sauce around the plate.

Chef's tip: Depending on the time available for presentation the hammour can be either served whole or cut into slices, as shown in the illustration.

66 *A delightfully simple and quick dish to prepare – which can be varied by using fresh herbs.* 99

Salmon en Croûte with Cucumber Confit
dill sauce

560 g to 600 g
fresh salmon,
filleted and
cleaned
220 ml white wine
cream sauce,
(see p 89)
2 tbsps chopped
dill
1 tsp lemon juice
1 onion, chopped
420 g cucumber,
grated
12 cherry
tomatoes
1 tbsp red wine
vinegar
1 tsp honey
400 g ready-made
puff pastry
1 egg, beaten
60 g butter
salt and pepper

Preparation time:
30 minutes
Cooking time:
30 minutes
Serves 4

For the filling

In a saucepan cook the onion with 30 g butter for 5 to 6 minutes. Then add the grated cucumber and continue cooking until all moisture has evaporated. Add the vinegar and honey and put aside.

For the sauce

Add the lemon juice with chopped dill to the white wine cream sauce. Whisk in the rest of the butter.

To prepare the croûte

1. Pre-heat the oven to 360°F/185°C/Gas Mark 4. On a lightly-floured surface roll out the pastry to a rectangular piece 50 x 25cm. Place on a large greased baking sheet.
2. Arrange the salmon on the lower half of the pastry rectangle leaving a 3cm border on the long edge and both sides. Spread the cucumber mixture over the fish.
3. Fold the 3cm border towards the fish, brush the pastry with beaten egg and fold over the top half of the pastry to completely enclose the salmon, sealing the edges well, tucking all around and under. Trim off any excess pastry.
4. Brush the croûte all over with beaten egg and bake in an oven for approx. 25 to 30 minutes or until the pastry is crispy and golden brown.

To serve, cut the pastry from both ends of the croûte and then divide into 4 equal portions. Place a slice in the centre of each plate, pour the sauce around this and garnish with cherry tomatoes.

❝*A delicious parcel of fish filled with a refreshing blend of cucumber and dill – perfect for summer dining.*❞

Sautéed Gulf Prawns with Couscous
saffron and red pepper sauce

20 medium-size
  prawns, approx.
  620 g, peeled
4 squid heads,
  cleaned and blanched
30 g butter
40 g mangetout,
  finely shredded
  and blanched

COUSCOUS
125 g instant couscous
240 ml vegetable stock,
  (see p 86)
20 ml olive oil
1 tsp chopped
  coriander
1 tsp chopped mint
salt and pepper

SAFFRON SAUCE
2 red peppers
2 shallots
80 ml white wine
1 clove garlic
30 g butter
60 ml olive oil
380 ml vegetable stock,
  (see p 86)
a pinch of saffron

Preparation time:
20 minutes
Cooking time:
15 minutes
Serves 4

Using a measuring jug as a guide, tip the couscous into a bowl. Add twice the volume of boiling vegetable stock. Mix in the olive oil and herbs and leave to absorb the liquid. This will take approx. 5 minutes.

Saffron sauce

1. Fry the finely chopped shallots and de-seeded and chopped red peppers with the olive oil for 5 minutes. Add the garlic, the saffron and white wine, then the vegetable stock and continue cooking for about 15 minutes.

2. Liquidise the sauce for about 30 seconds and return to the stove.

3. If the sauce is a little thick, add more stock until it reaches the right pouring consistency. Pass through a fine sieve and whisk in the butter. Check the seasoning and keep warm.

4. Heat the remaining butter in a pan and quickly fry the prawns for 4 to 5 minutes.

To serve, put a small bowl of couscous in the middle of each plate and place a squid on top arranging the prawns around it. Pour the sauce around the plate and garnish with the mangetout.

Chef's tip: Different varieties of saffron are cheaply available from the spice souks.

“ *This delectable seafood dish has a plethora of Middle Eastern flavours; the fresh seafood catch, the rich enhancement of saffron and the refreshing accompaniment of couscous.* ”

Steamed Red Snapper Fillets with Blue Crab
coconut curry sauce

4 red snapper fillets
4 fresh blue crabs
4 bok-choy leaves, green part only, blanched
1 shallot, chopped
2 spring onions, shredded
½ tsp ginger, chopped
a pinch of Chinese five-spices
1 tsp light soy sauce
2 tbsps mayonnaise, (see p 88)
30 g butter

CURRY SAUCE
40 g butter
2 shallots,
1 stalk of lemon grass,
½ tsp ginger
1 clove garlic,
4 lime leaves, shredded
a pinch of saffron
1 tsp medium curry powder
120 ml white wine
260 ml fish stock, (see p 86)
80 ml coconut milk

Preparation time:
40 minutes
Cooking time:
10 minutes
Serves 4

1. Cook the crab for 8 minutes in boiling water and strain. When cold remove the meat from body.

2. Heat the butter in a frying pan and add the ginger and shallots. Cook gently until transparent.

3. Add the crabmeat with the soy sauce and Chinese spices and cook for a few seconds. Transfer to a bowl and add the mayonnaise. Keep aside.

For the sauce

1. Heat the 30 g butter in a saucepan and add the chopped shallot, ginger, garlic, lemon grass, lime leaves and saffron. Cook for 2 to 3 minutes.

2. Add the curry powder and cook for a further minute before adding the wine. Reduce until all the liquid has evaporated then add the fish stock and coconut milk and simmer for 30 minutes.

3. Strain into a small saucepan and continue reducing to a smooth consistency. Whisk in the remaining butter and keep warm.

To assemble

Sandwich the crab mixture between the two fillets of fish. Neatly place a bok-choy leaf around the middle of the sandwiched fillets. Arrange the fish in a steamed basket. Place the steamer over a pan of boiling water, cover and steam for 10 to 12 minutes.

To serve, arrange the fish in the middle of each plate, and spoon the sauce around the fish.

"This rich fish course relies upon the specific sauce ingredients for its distinctive Far Eastern flavour that suits the firm flesh of red snapper."

Fisherman's Catch
coriander and cumin sauce

approx. 180 g
  seafood for each
  person
(prawn, red mullet,
  salmon, hammour,
  mussels, monkfish,
  lobster)
4 pastry trellis,
  (see p 93)
4 crayfish

THE SAUCE
2 shallots, finely
  chopped
120 ml dry white
  wine
250 ml fish stock,
  (see p 86)
100 ml cream
60 g butter
a pinch of cayenne
a pinch of cumin
  powder
2 tbsps of
  coriander,
  chopped
a few drops of
  lemon juice
salt and pepper

Preparation time:
30 minutes
Cooking time:
10 minutes
Serves 4

A selection of about six to eight varieties of shellfish is needed for this dish. But use what is available to you.

1. Pre-heat the oven to 375°F/190°C/Gas Mark 5. Trim the fish fillets and remove bones then cut into bite-size pieces. Grease an ovenproof dish with 10 g butter and scatter the fish and shellfish into it.
2. Add the chopped shallots, the wine and fish stock and lay a sheet of greaseproof paper over the whole dish. Cook in the oven for 8 to 10 minutes only.
3. Take the fish from the oven and gently remove it from the stock and keep warm. Strain the stock into a saucepan and boil until reduced by three-quarters. Add the cream and reduce to a pouring consistency. Whisk in the remaining butter, the cumin powder, herbs, cayenne and lemon juice. Season.
4. Arrange the seafood attractively on warmed plates and spoon the sauce over.

Chef's tip: In the illustration a trellis basket (see p 93) and crayfish have been placed on top for presentation and are options which the more daring cook can attempt!

❝ *This extravagantly presented dish will suit individual tastes, as it can be prepared with an infinite combination of fish and seafood. The light, creamy sauce gently complements the seafood and leaves the palate fresh.* ❞

Parrot Fish with Pistachio Herb Crust

8 x 80 g to 90 g parrot
 fish fillets
120 ml white wine
80 ml fish stock,
 (see p 86)
pistachio herb crust,
 (see p 92)

**RED PEPPER AND
TOMATO COULIS**

1 red pepper, skinned
 and finely diced
3 tomatoes, skinned,
 seeded and finely
 chopped
2 shallots, finely diced
1 clove of garlic,
 chopped
1 tsp tapenade,
 (see p 93)
30 ml olive oil
60 ml water
salt and pepper

*Preparation time:
40 minutes
Cooking time:
25 minutes
Serves 4*

For the coulis

1. Place the red pepper under a hot grill or gas flame and cook for 10 to 12 minutes, turning frequently, until the skin is charred and black. Cool slightly, then peel off skin under the cold tap.

2. Cook the shallots and the red pepper in olive oil for 3 to 4 minutes.

3. Add garlic, chopped tomatoes and water. Cook until it becomes a paste. Add tapenade and season.

Baking the fish

1. Pre-heat the oven to 400°F/200°C/Gas Mark 6. Prepare the pistachio herb crust.

2. Spread a layer of tomato and pepper coulis on half of the fish fillets and a coating of pistachio crust on the remaining 4 fillets.

3. Lay the dressed fish side by side in an ovenproof baking dish and pour in the white wine and stock. Bring to boil on top of the stove and then place in the oven for 6 to 8 minutes.

To serve, place the fillets with tomato coulis on a serving plate and arrange the fish with the nut crust on top but at an angle as shown in the illustration. Pour remaining juices from the cooking dish around the plate and garnish with a bouquet of vegetables.

Chef's tip: Parrot fish becomes very soft upon cooking and requires delicate handling.

66 *The natural juices contribute to the wonderful melt-in-the-mouth texture of this layered fish dish.* 99

Omani Lobster Thermidor
Parmesan cheese crust

2 live lobsters
each weighing
560 to 700 g
320 ml bechamel,
(see p 91)
1 onion, finely
chopped
220 g mushrooms,
sliced
240 ml white wine
60 ml brandy
160 ml cream
1 tbsp mustard
2 tsps tarragon
80 g butter
60 g Parmesan or
grated cheddar
cheese

Preparation time:
30 minutes
Cooking time:
15 minutes
Serves 2

1. Pre-heat the oven to 400°F/200°C/Gas Mark 6. Plunge the whole lobsters in boiling water and cook for 2 minutes. Remove them and refresh in ice water.

2. Split the lobsters in two and remove the meat.

3. Return the empty shells to the boiling water and cook a further 6 minutes. Drain and set aside.

4. Cut the lobster meat into bite-size pieces.

5. In a frying pan heat 30 g butter, add half the lobster meat and cook on a high heat for no more than 2 minutes. Flame with brandy and strain into a bowl reserving the juices. Repeat with the remaining lobster.

6. Heat 30 g butter in a saucepan, add the onion and cook until transparent. Add the mushrooms and continue cooking until the liquid has evaporated.

7. Add the white wine and reduce the liquid by approx. half. Now add the cream, mustard, herbs and the bechamel. Cook until thickened. Fold the lobster meat into the sauce and add the remaining butter.

8. Fill the lobster shells with this mixture. Sprinkle with grated Parmesan or cheddar and brown in a hot oven.

Chef's tip: Cigalis are a successful substitute for lobster, when in season.

❝*A true classic – this dish is offered to guests throughout the year and I am frequently asked how it is prepared; it gives me pleasure to share this great favourite.*❞

Chicken Breast with Salmon
asparagus and shrimps

4 x 160 g to 180 g
skinless chicken
breasts
140 g salmon fillet
120 g cocktail prawns
40 g clarified butter
12 asparagus tips
180 ml white wine
280 ml chicken stock,
reduced to 6 tbsps,
(see p 86)
160 ml cream
salt and pepper

Preparation time:
30 minutes
Cooking time:
15 minutes
Serves 4

1. Pre-heat the oven to 400°F/200°C/Gas Mark 6.

2. Peel and cook the asparagus in salted boiling water for approx. 10 minutes. Refresh in cold water. Drain and cut diagonally into 1in pieces.

3. Dice the salmon into small cubes, season with salt and pepper and mix with a little of the cream.

4. Lay the chicken breast with the inside facing you. Pull away the inner fillet without detaching it and bat this out lightly with a meat hammer or rolling pin.

5. Place 1 large tbsp of the salmon mixture on each breast, then fold over the inner fillet so that it is completely enclosed.

6. Season the chicken breasts and seal in a hot pan with the clarified butter. Then place in the oven for approx. 12 to 15 minutes or until firm to the touch. Remove from the oven and keep warm.

7. Pan-fry the cocktail prawns and asparagus in the same pan for a few seconds. Set aside.

8. Pour the wine in the pan and reduce by about half. Now add the chicken stock and the remaining cream and reduce to a light coating consistency.

To serve, arrange the chicken on each serving plate, either whole or thinly sliced and spoon the sauce over or around, then garnish with the prawns and some asparagus tips.

Chef's tip: For a less extravagant dish, the salmon may be omitted.

" Tender chicken with the additional
elegance of salmon and a creamy sauce – a dish both simple
to prepare and assemble. **"**

Pan-fried Calf's Liver with Kumquats
potato bhaji

550 g calf's liver,
  cut into 8 slices
80 g butter
260 ml dark sauce,
  (see p 90)
1 tsp honey
juice of 1 orange
80 ml basic
  vinaigrette (see p 87)
16 kumquats
1/2 leek, white part,
  shredded

250 g potato, cut
  into julienne
200 g cabbage, finely
  shredded
3 slices of back bacon,
  cut into julienne
2 onions, finely sliced
25 g coriander leaves,
  chopped
1/2 tsp each of
  coriander powder,
  cumin powder,
  turmeric powder,
  mustard seed,
  chilli powder and
  cumin seed
60 ml corn oil

Preparation time:
25 minutes
Cooking time:
15 minutes
Serves 4

1. Cook the kumquats with 60 g sugar in 140 ml water for 10 minutes. When cool cut each one in half.
2. Remove any threads from the liver and season each piece.
3. Heat 40 g butter in a frying pan over a medium heat. When the butter is foaming, cook half the liver for 2 minutes on each side. Deglaze the pan with half the orange juice and pour into a bowl. Quickly wipe out the pan with kitchen paper and cook the remaining liver as before.
4. Deglaze the pan with the remaining orange juice, honey, and dark sauce. Add the kumquats, stirring all the time. Cook until the sauce has reached a pouring consistency and add the vinaigrette.

Potato bhaji
Heat the oil in a wide shallow pan until very hot. Place the mustard and cumin seed in the pan and cook for a minute. Then add all other spices and cook for a further minute until the flavours have blended together. Then add the onion, potato, bacon and cabbage, and cook for 10 to 15 minutes, stirring occasionally. Garnish with coriander leaves.

To serve, divide the potato bhaji among the 4 serving plates. Place 2 or 3 slices of calf's liver on top of the potato and pour the sauce over. Garnish with the deep-fried leek.

Chef's tip: Be cautious when cooking the liver, as it becomes rubbery very quickly and should be served soon after cooking.

❝The spicy, smoked bacon bhaji makes a perfect
platter for the tender calf's liver; the kumquats
add a surprising sweetness.❞

Roast Loin of Lamb with Onion Confit
red wine sauce with black olives

MARINADE
1 tsp honey
2 tsps soy sauce
juice of $^1/_4$ lemon
a pinch of Chinese
* five spices*
1 tsp paprika
1 tsp basil
1 tsp tarragon
60 ml sunflower
* oil*

4 loins of lamb
250 ml red wine
* sauce (see p 92)*
20 g butter
120 g black olives,
* sliced*

ONION CONFIT
450 g onions,
* thinly sliced*
40 g butter
20 g oil
2 tbsps red wine
vinegar
salt and pepper

Preparation time:
30 minutes
Cooking time:
10 minutes
Serves 4

Lamb marinade

1. Mix together the marinade ingredients, season with salt and pepper.

2. Marinate the fillets of lamb for 6 hours or overnight.

Onion confit

Heat the butter with oil in a wide-based pan. Add the onions and cook gently for 30 minutes, stirring occasionally until the onions are tender. Stir in the vinegar and continue cooking on a low heat until the mixture becomes concentrated and 'jammy'. Season.

Preparing the lamb

1. Pre-heat the oven to 400°F/200°C/Gas Mark 6. Seal the lamb on a high heat for 1 minute in a pan or roasting dish and transfer to the oven for 8 to 10 minutes, depending on how well you like the lamb cooked.

2. Remove from the oven and allow to rest for 10 minutes before serving. Deglaze the roasting dish with the red wine sauce.

3. Add the olives and whisk in 20 g butter.

To serve, divide the onions among the 4 serving plates. Cut each loin portion into slices and arrange these on the onions in a fan shape. Pour the sauce around the lamb and garnish with a bouquet of vegetables.

Chef's tip: When selecting the joint of lamb, get the butcher to trim off all the fat and sinew from the best end of lamb. Retain all the trimmings and bones for the stock.

66 *The special blend of spices and tarragon in
the marinade provide a bouquet of flavours which
are sealed within the tender roast lamb.* 99

Veal Medallions with Lobster Skewers
chive cream and pasta

1 veal fillet
  (approx. 540 g)
200 g lobster tail
180 g fresh pasta
  cut into linguine,
  (see p 90)
260 ml chicken
  stock (see p 86)
120 ml white wine
2 finely chopped
  shallots
60 g butter
30 ml oil
180 ml cream
2 tbsps chives, chopped
12 blanched courgettes,

LOBSTER MARINADE
60 ml hot chilli sauce
$^1/_2$ clove garlic,
  chopped
a pinch of cumin
  powder
a pinch of coriander
  powder
2 tbsps corn oil
juice of $^1/_2$ lemon

Preparation time:
30 minutes
Cooking time:
8 minutes
Serves 4

Marinade
Mix all the marinade ingredients together and season.
Remove the lobster meat from the shell, cut into cubes
of 2sq cm each and thread 2 to 3 cubes on to 7cm wooden
barbecue skewers, allowing 3 skewers per person.

1. Sweat the finely chopped shallots in 20 g butter for a
few minutes.
2. Add the wine and reduce by half, then add the stock and
reduce again until approx. 6 tbsps of liquid remain. Add the
cream and simmer until reduced to a coating consistency.
Pass through a fine sieve. Add the chopped chives and
whisk in 20 g of the remaining butter.
3. Cook the linguine in a pan of boiling salted water for 2
minutes and drain. Warm the courgettes for a few seconds.
4. Trim the veal fillet and cut into 12 pieces. Season the veal
fillets and sauté in hot butter in a frying pan for 2 minutes
on each side. Remove from the pan and keep warm.
5. Heat the oil in a frying pan and cook the skewered
lobster for approx. 1 minute.

To serve, pour the sauce on to each plate, and arrange 3
veal fillets in a triangular shape. Place the pasta in the
middle and top each fillet with a skewer of lobster. Garnish
with courgettes.

66 *Seafood accompanies veal very well and this dish would adapt well to being cooked on a barbecue.* 99

Roast Guinea-fowl with Baby Onion Jus
mushroom and herb stuffing

2 guinea-fowls, each weighing approx. 800 g
1 carrot, chopped
1 large onion, chopped
220 g shallots
2 cloves garlic
320 ml dark sauce, (see p 90)
120 ml chicken stock (see p 86)
salt and pepper

MUSHROOM STUFFING
320 g field mushrooms, cleaned and sliced
2 chopped shallots
1 clove garlic, chopped
90 g butter
4 tbsps chopped mixed herbs
80 ml white wine
salt and pepper

Preparation time:
30 minutes
Cooking time:
25 minutes
Serves 4

To make the stuffing
1. Heat 30 g butter in a pan and sweat the shallots for 2 minutes until transparent. Add the mushrooms and cook until the juices have evaporated.
2. Then add the garlic, white wine, herbs and cook until the liquid has completely evaporated. Season with salt and pepper.
3. Transfer to a food processor and blend for 30 seconds. When cool, add the remaining butter. Mix well and set aside.

For the guinea-fowl
1. Pre-heat the oven to 400°F/200°C/Gas Mark 6. Gently ease the skin from the end part of the breast of each bird and pipe the mushroom stuffing into the cavity and smooth out evenly.
2. Season the birds and seal in a hot roasting pan with oil. Add the carrot, onion, and garlic and place in the oven for 20 to 25 minutes. Remove from the oven and keep warm.
3. Deglaze the pan with the stock and add the dark sauce. Reduce for a few minutes, skim off the fat and pass through a sieve into a saucepan. Add the shallots and season to taste.

To serve, cut the guinea-fowl in half, remove the breast bones and place in the centre of each plate. Coat with the hot sauce.

Chef's tip: To remove the shallot skins more easily, blanch them whole in boiling water for 3 minutes. The skins will peel off without effort.

❝The rich, aromatic appeal of this dish is achieved by the mushroom stuffing which ensures the guinea-fowl retains its natural juices through cooking.❞

Duck Breast with Grapes and Redcurrants

2 ducks weighing
approx. 2.3 kg
140 g white grapes,
*   peeled*
120 g redcurrants

THE SAUCE
duck carcasses
1 onion, chopped
1 carrot, chopped
300 ml white wine
60 ml grape juice
2 tbsps raspberry
*   vinegar*
1 tbsp redcurrant
*   jelly*
350 ml dark sauce,
*   (see p 90)*
600 ml water
20 g butter
40 ml oil
a few sprigs of
*   redcurrants for*
*   decoration*

Preparation time:
40 minutes
Cooking time:
20 minutes
Serves 4

1. Remove 4 duck breasts and reserve the legs for another recipe or freeze for later use but retain the carcasses. Pre-heat the oven to 380°F/195°C/Gas Mark 5. Chop the duck carcasses into small pieces. Brown the vegetables in a deep roasting pan with oil for a few minutes, then add the carcasses. Place in the oven for 15 to 20 minutes.

2. Transfer the pan from the oven to the hob and remove the fat. Then add the vinegar and wine. Bring to the boil, removing the sediment from the pan. Add the water and simmer for 30 minutes.

3. Strain through a sieve into a saucepan and reduce the liquid by half.

4. Add the dark sauce, grape juice and the redcurrant jelly. Continue reducing until the sauce coats the back of a spoon.

5. Strain once more and whisk in the butter. Add the grapes and redcurrants. Check seasoning.

For the duck breast

Heat a roasting pan on the hob and fry the duck breasts skin side down for 2 minutes. Turn the breasts over and place the pan in the oven to cook for approx. 8 to 10 minutes. This will depend on the size of the breasts but they should remain pink in the centre. Remove from the pan and rest for 10 minutes before serving.

To serve, slice each breast and arrange neatly on each plate. Pour the sauce either on top of the breasts or around the plate.

❝*Tasty accompaniments to this succulent duck recipe include potato dauphinois, a medley of vegetables as a garnish and the tangy flavour of redcurrants.*❞

Beef Tournedos with Roquefort Ravioli
red wine sauce and walnuts

600 g beef fillet, cut
into 4 tournedos
140 g ratatouille,
(see p 87)
130 g fresh pasta,
(see p 90)
200 ml red wine
sauce (see p 92)
40 ml brandy
160 g Roquefort
cheese
4 basil leaves,
chopped
2 tbsps cream
60 g walnuts
60 g butter

Preparation time:
20 minutes
Cooking time:
8 minutes
Serves 4

1. Blend the Roquefort with the cream and basil. Set aside.
2. Roll out the pasta as thinly as possible on a floured surface. Cut into 8 rounds using a 6cm cutter.
3. Place 1 tbsp of the cheese filling in the centre of 4 of the rounds. Brush the edges of the pasta with water and place the remaining 4 rounds on top, to make individual ravioli portions. Seal carefully and set aside.
4. Warm the ratatouille.
5. Melt half of the butter in a frying pan and heat until foaming and golden. Add the steaks and cook on both sides until medium rare. This will take approx. 4 to 6 minutes. Transfer to a plate and keep warm.
6. Pour the brandy into the pan, scraping the base with a wooden spoon. Add the red wine and walnuts and reduce for a while. Season and whisk in the rest of the butter.
7. Cook the ravioli in boiling water for 2 minutes.

To serve, place a tournedos in the centre of each plate. Pour the sauce on top, then add 1 tbsp of ratatouille on top of the tournedos. To finish, put the ravioli on top of this. Serve with a selection of vegetables.

Chef's tip: To retain the whiteness of the walnuts, blanch them for 2 to 3 minutes, remove the skins and leave the nuts to soak in a bowl of milk.

❝ *When the ravioli is cut into, the Roquefort immediately melts with the tender beef. A surprise combination.* ❞

Lamb Noisettes with Boursin and Mint Parcel
chilli piquant jus

4 loins of lamb,
  approx. 160 g each,
  boned and trimmed
360 g chicken mousse,
  (see p 92)
600 ml chicken stock,
  (see p 86)
80 g Boursin cheese
  with garlic
1 leaf of leek, blanched
3 tsps mint leaves,
  chopped
2 tbsps cream
30 g leaves of spinach,
  cooked and drained
12 saffron potatoes
2 tbsps cornflour
3 egg whites
salt and pepper

CHILLI SAUCE
300 g ripe tomatoes,
  chopped
160 ml dark sauce,
  (see p 90)
1 onion, chopped
60 ml olive oil
1 clove garlic, chopped
2 tsps red chilli sauce
salt and pepper

Preparation time:
45 minutes
Cooking time:
15 minutes
Serves 4

For the parcel
1. Mix the cornflour in a bowl with the egg whites and 60 ml water. Make 4 to 6 very thin pancakes in a 14cm non-stick pan with the butter. Season.
2. Blend the Boursin with the chopped mint and the cream. Refrigerate for 30 minutes.
3. Lay 4 pancakes on a flat surface and place 1 tbsp of the cheese mixture in the centre of each pancake. Bring the edges up to enclose the filling and shape into a parcel. Tie the neck of the bag with a strip of leek.

For the sauce
Heat the oil in a saucepan, add the onion and garlic for a few minutes. Add the tomatoes, red chilli and dark sauces. Continue cooking for 20 minutes until the tomatoes have softened. Remove from the heat and pass the sauce through a fine sieve. Season and set aside.

To assemble
Season the lamb fillets. Prepare the mousse adding the cooked spinach. Spread the chicken mousse very thinly all over the fillet and roll up into a sausage with the clingfilm. Tie the ends and leave aside. Bring the chicken stock to boil and poach the 'sausage' in this for 8 to 10 minutes. Remove from the stock and leave to rest for 8 minutes before serving. Deep-fry the cheese parcels for 2 minutes until crisp.

To serve, remove the clingfilm from the lamb and cut each into 3 noisettes. Arrange the lamb in the centre of each plate and place a parcel in the middle of these. Pour the hot sauce around the plate and garnish with the saffron potatoes.

❝The simple method of boiling the sealed lamb results in the stunning contrast of pink meat and bright green spinach in the chicken mousse.❞

Crème Brûlée Tart with Raspberries

260 g fresh
  raspberries
200 g sweet pastry,
  (see p 94)
350 ml double cream
5 egg yolks
60 g sugar
6 tbsps demerara or
  white sugar
lemon crème anglaise,
  (see p 95)
fruit coulis (see p 95)

Preparation time:
45 minutes
Cooking time:
1 ½ hours
Serves 4 to 5

1. Pre-heat the oven to 275°F/140°C/Gas Mark 1.
2. Put the cream into a large saucepan and bring to the boil over a low heat. In a large bowl whisk the sugar and egg yolks until pale and add the cream.
3. Cook the custard mixture over a low heat, stirring with a wooden spoon. The custard must not boil or it will curdle. As soon as bubbles start to appear, remove from the heat and pour through a fine sieve into a jug.
4. Pour the custard into an approx. 18cm-wide and 5cm-high ovenproof dish and place in a roasting tin. Pour hot water into the tin to come halfway up the side of the dish.
5. Bake for approx. 1¼ hours or until the custard is set. Leave to cool and refrigerate for 3 hours before filling the tart.

To make the tart

1. Pre-heat the oven to 400°F/200°C/Gas Mark 6. Roll out the pastry on a lightly floured surface to a thickness of 5mm and cut out four 12cm circles. Line four 10cm ring-moulds with the pastry, trimming any excess dough.
2. Place each mould on a baking tray, line the insides with a circle of greaseproof paper and weigh down with baking beans. Leave to rest in a refrigerator for 15 minutes.
3. Bake in the oven for 10 minutes then remove the beans and paper and continue to bake for approx. 5 to 8 more minutes until light golden brown. Cool on a wire tray, then remove the rings.
4. Fill the pastry cases to the rims with the custard. Sprinkle an even layer of sugar on top and place under a hot grill until caramelised.

66Delightfully individual desserts, with fresh raspberries temptingly arranged on top of the crème brûlée, encircled in lemon crème anglaise and fruit coulis. 99

Cold Lemon Soufflé
chocolate cointreau sabayon

250 ml milk
25 g cornflour
2 eggs, separated
65 g caster sugar
juice and zest
 of 1 lemon
6 finger biscuits
4 tbsps sugar
syrup (2 tbsps of
 sugar with 2
 tbsps of water)
2 tbsps Cointreau
15 g butter

SABAYON
3 egg yolks
100 g caster sugar
2 tsps cocoa
2 tbsps Cointreau
6 tbsps white wine
 or water

Preparation time:
35 minutes
Cooking time:
20 minutes
Serves 4 to 5

1. Pre-heat the oven to 380°F/195°C/Gas Mark 5. Grease four 8cm x 5cm soufflé dishes well with the butter and sprinkle with 10 g sugar inside the dishes to coat, tipping out any excess.

2. Soak the sponge fingers in the sugar syrup and Cointreau.

3. Gently heat the milk in a saucepan with the lemon zest.

4. Whisk the egg yolks and remaining 50 g sugar in a separate bowl until light and thick. Add the cornflour and mix well.

5. Pour the milk over the mixture whisking constantly and return to the pan. Cook over a low heat, stirring all the time until the mixture thickens. Add the lemon juice and cook for another minute. Cool.

6. Beat the egg whites with the rest of the sugar, until stiff but not dry and gently fold them into the yolk mixture.

7. Half fill the soufflé dishes with lemon mixture and then place a layer of the finger biscuits on this. Now fill the dishes to the rims with more lemon soufflé. Scrape a palette knife over the dishes to level.

8. Place in a roasting pan half filled with hot water and bake in an oven for 15 to 20 minutes. Place in the fridge for 2 hours.

For the sabayon
Place all the ingredients in a bowl over a pan of simmering water. Whisk briskly for 5 minutes until the mixture begins to thicken. Remove from the heat and continue whisking until the sabayon has cooled.

To serve, remove the soufflé from the dishes and place one in the centre of each plate. Decorate as shown in the illustration.

66 *Lemon soufflé is an internationally renowned dessert,*
and here the rich addition of chocolate sabayon makes this a
sweet hard to resist. 99

Carrot and Nut Bars

300 g carrots,
  grated
150 g caster sugar
6 eggs, separated
100 g almonds,
  chopped
50 g walnuts,
  chopped
75 g ground
  almonds
a pinch of
  cinnamon
1 tsp baking
  powder
200 g cream
  cheese
200 g yoghurt
2 leaves gelatine
120 g apricot
  halves, tinned

Preparation time:
35 minutes
Cooking time:
45 minutes
Serves 8

1. Pre-heat the oven to 350°F/180°C/Gas Mark 4. Grease a 24sq cm x 3cm-high non-stick tin.

2. Soak the gelatine in a little water.

3. Place the egg yolks and sugar in a bowl and using an electric mixer beat until light in colour.

4. Fold in the grated carrots, nuts, ground almonds, baking powder and the pinch of cinnamon until blended.

5. Whisk the egg whites until stiff but not dry and fold into the cake mixture using a spatula.

6. Pour the batter into the prepared tin and bake for 45 to 50 minutes.

7. Remove from the oven and leave to cool. Turn out on to a flat tray.

8. Remove the gelatine from the water and melt in a microwave for a few seconds or stir in a bowl until dissolved.

9. Mix the cream cheese with the yoghurt and blend in the gelatine. Spread over the top of the cake.

10. To obtain the coulis, purée the apricot with its syrup in a blender. Pass through a sieve.

To serve, place a slice of the cake on a plate and decorate with the apricot coulis.

66*A perfectly moist cake, ideal for picnics.*99

Date and Chocolate Délice

240 g good quality
plain chocolate
180 g butter,
softened
4 egg yolks
240 ml whipping
cream
80 g sugar
200 g dates,
stoned, skinned
and chopped

GLAZE
130 g plain
chocolate, melted
150 ml cream

Preparation time:
25 minutes
Serves 6

1. Line a baking dish with greaseproof paper and place 6 individual ring moulds on the paper. Tightly pack the bottom of each mould with dates.

2. Break the chocolate into pieces and melt in a small heatproof bowl over a pan of simmering water.

3. Stir the softened butter into the chocolate and blend until smooth. Then remove the bowl from the pan and add the egg yolks, mixing well.

4. Whip the cream with the sugar until it holds its shape.

5. Fold the cream lightly into the chocolate mixture taking care not to overmix.

6. Fill the prepared ring moulds with the chocolate mousse. Chill for 1 hour.

7. Make the glaze by blending the chocolate with the warmed cream until smooth and glossy. Then, glaze the top of the prepared chocolate mousse.

To serve, carefully remove the mousse from the ring mould by heating a knife in hot water and running it around the inside edge of the mould. Place the mousse on the plate and decorate as you like.

Chef's tip: Keep the mousse out of the fridge for 20 minutes before serving as it should be served at room temperature.

66 *A sophisticated chocolate mousse enriched with the local delicacy of fresh dates.* **99**

Parfait Moka
chocolate sauce

140 g caster sugar
5 egg yolks
250 ml whipping
  cream
3 tsps instant
  coffee granules
4 tbsps brandy
50 ml water

THE SAUCE
175 g good quality
  plain chocolate
260 ml cream
140 ml water

*Preparation time:
25 minutes
Serves 8 to 10*

1. Line a 1 x 1 litre loaf tin with clingfilm. Gently heat the sugar and water in a saucepan until dissolved. Boil for 2 minutes.

2. In a bowl beat the egg yolks with the coffee granules and the brandy with an electric hand mixer. Then pour the hot sugar syrup onto the yolks in a steady stream, whisking all the time. Increase the speed of the mixer and continue whisking for 6 to 8 minutes until the mixture has doubled in volume and is thick and foamy. Reduce to a medium speed until the mixture has cooled slightly.

3. Whip the cream until it holds its shape and gently fold into the mixture. For a marble effect swirl 4 tbsps of the chocolate sauce (see below) into the mixture before pouring into the loaf tin.

4. Freeze for approx. 4 to 6 hours until firm.

For the chocolate sauce
Break the chocolate into a saucepan and add the cream and water. Warm gently, stirring continuously until the chocolate has melted and thickened slightly.

To serve, pour the chocolate sauce in the centre of the plate. Arrange a slice of parfait moka on top and decorate as you like.

Chef's tip: The illustration shows this frozen dessert has been served in the form of a block.

A creamy, bitter-sweet combination.

Coupe Le Classique

460 g fresh
  strawberries,
  hulled
80 g raspberries
80 g blueberries
4 filo pastry cases,
  (see p 94)
400 ml fresh
  cream
120 ml fromage
  frais
40 ml Grand
  Marnier
140 g icing sugar
chocolate for
  decoration

MERINGUE
2 egg whites
110 g caster sugar

Preparation time:
20 minutes
Cooking time:
1 hour
Serves 4

1. Pre-heat the oven to 270°F/135°C/Gas Mark 1.
Whisk the egg whites until they form soft peaks. Add the
sugar and continue to whisk for 2 to 3 minutes.
2. Place 2 rounded tbsps of the mixture on a greaseproof-
lined baking sheet and place in the oven for 1 hour. Turn
off the heat and leave overnight to dry out.

To assemble

1. Chop half the strawberries and place in a blender with
the icing sugar. Liquidise to a purée and pass through a
sieve to remove the seeds. Reserve 3 tbsps.
2. Chop the remaining strawberries and mix with the
other fruits.
3. Whip the cream to the floppy stage and gently fold in the
fromage frais.
4. Roughly break the meringues. Place in a large mixing
bowl and add the fruits. Fold in the cream and purée to
give a marbled effect.
5. Spoon the cream filling into the filo cases and drizzle the
remaining purée around the plate. Decorate with grated
chocolate. Serve immediately.

Chef's tip: Instead of pastry cases,
sundae dishes can be used for this
dessert.

A deliciously light ensemble of soft berries with an appetising crunch of meringue.

Apple Millefeuille with Mascarpone Cheese
caramel and calvados sauce

100 g butter,
 melted
250 g puff pastry,
 ready-made
1 tbsp icing sugar
60 g caster sugar
5 eating apples
220 g Mascarpone
 cheese
100 ml whipped
 cream
juice and zest of
 1 lemon
4 sprigs of mint

CARAMEL SAUCE
60 g caster sugar
40 ml water
240 ml cream

Preparation time:
40 minutes
Cooking time:
10 minutes
Serves 4

1. Pre-heat the oven to 400°F/200°C/Gas Mark 6. In a saucepan, dissolve the sugar with water over low heat. Then cook on a high heat until the sugar turns a deep amber colour. Immediately turn off the heat and whisk in the cream. Simmer for 2 minutes and strain. Keep aside.

2. Roll out the puff pastry with a pasta machine to 4 rectangles measuring 30cm x 8cm. Chill for 15 minutes to relax the pastry.

3. Sprinkle the pastry with icing sugar and bake for 6 to 10 minutes. When cool, neatly cut out 12 circles with a 7cm pastry cutter. You will require 3 for each dessert.

4. Mix together the Mascarpone cheese, cream, lemon zest and 2 tbsps of the lemon juice. Cover and chill for 1 hour.

5. Peel and core the apples. Using a melon baller scoop out 48 apple balls. Heat the butter in a frying-pan and sauté the apples in two batches until translucent, approx. 4 to 6 minutes. Set aside.

6. Put the caster sugar into the same pan with the lemon juice and cook until it begins to colour. Add the apple balls and fry on a high heat until all the apples have caramelised.

To assemble

Fill a piping bag fitted with a No. 5 nozzle with the Mascarpone cream. Place 6 apple balls around the edge of 4 of the pastry circles and pipe rosettes between the balls. Repeat the process with the remaining apples and pastry circles ending with a pastry circle. Dust liberally with icing sugar. Heat the metal skewer over a gas flame and mark out diamond pattern lines. Carefully lift the finished millefeuilles on to the dessert plates and pour the sauce around. Garnish with apple slices and a sprig of mint.

66Apples are the ideal fruit for caramelising and for this dessert they create a mouth-watering contrast with layers of light pastry. 99

Peach Melba en Cage

5 ripe peaches, cut
 into halves
500 ml water
360 g caster sugar
175 g fresh or
 frozen
 raspberries
juice of ½ lemon
260 ml fresh
 cream, whipped
360 ml crème
 anglaise,
 (see p 95)
mint leaves
pastry trellis,
 (see p 93)

Preparation time:
35 minutes
Serves 4

To poach the peaches

1. Dissolve the sugar in the water and bring to the boil.

2. Add the peach halves and simmer gently for 8 to 10 minutes. Test with a skewer for tenderness.

3. Remove from the heat and allow to cool in the liquid.

4. Place 2 peach halves in the blender with some of the syrup and mix into a purée. Pass through a fine sieve and chill before use.

For the ice-cream

Whip the cream into the crème anglaise. Place in an ice-cream machine and churn until frozen.

For the raspberry coulis

Place the raspberries and 100 g sugar in a blender and mix into a purée. Pass through a fine sieve and add the lemon juice. Chill before use.

To serve, place a disc of ice-cream in the centre of a soup plate. Arrange a trellis cup on top of this and put half a peach into the cup. Fill the cavity of the peach with whipping cream and sandwich with another peach half. Carefully enclose the peach with a second cup. Surround the cage with both the peach and raspberry coulis, a few raspberries and the mint leaves.

Chef's tip: If you don't have an ice-cream machine use a top quality vanilla ice-cream.

66A special variation of the ever-popular peach melba.
The smooth ice-cream base refreshingly complements the
crispy trellis. 99

66 *I believe the overall appeal of a dish lies in serving the food with a special sauce – and I give particular attention to the ingredients that go into each, not least the freshest vegetables and fruit, which are always available from the Gulf markets.* 99

Sauces & Sundries

Bechamel Sauce *91*

Butter Sauce or Beurre Blanc *89*

Chicken Mousse *92*

Chicken Stock *86*

Cocktail Sauce *88*

Crème Anglaise *95*

Dark Sauce *90*

Filo Pastry Cases *91*

Fish Stock *86*

Fresh Pasta *90*

Fruit Coulis *95*

Mayonnaise *88*

Pastry Trellis *93*

Pesto *88*

Pistachio Herb Crust *92*

Ratatouille *87*

Red Wine Sauce *92*

Sweet Pastry *91*

Tapenade *93*

Tomato Coulis *87*

Tomato Sauce *91*

Vegetable Stock *86*

Basic Vinaigrette *87*

White Wine Cream Sauce *89*

Fish Stock
Makes approx. 1 litre

1.5 kg fish bones, chopped • 2 carrots, chopped • 1 large onion, chopped
• 2 celery sticks, sliced • 1 leek, sliced • 1/2 fennel bulb, chopped
• 1 bouquet garni (thyme, parsley, bay leaf) • 300 ml white wine • 2 1/2 litres of water
• 10 black peppercorns • 60 g butter

1. Wash the fish bones. Heat the oil in a saucepan and cook the vegetables gently for a few minutes until soft.
2. Add the bones and cook for a few more minutes before adding the white wine and water, bring to the boil, then skim.
3. Simmer for 20 minutes.
4. Pass through a strainer or fine sieve, leave to cool.
5. Store in the fridge for not more than 2 or 3 days or freeze.

Vegetable Stock
Makes approx. 1.5 litres

60 g butter • 1 onion, chopped • 1 carrot, diced • 1 leek, chopped
• 1 turnip, diced • mushroom peelings • 2 celery sticks, chopped • 1 fennel bulb, chopped
• 1 clove garlic • 1 3/4 litre water • 10 peppercorns • 1 bouquet garni

1. Sweat the vegetables in the butter in a large saucepan for 5 minutes until soft.
2. Add the water, peppercorn and bouquet garni, and bring to the boil, simmer for 25 minutes.
3. Strain the stock through a fine sieve squeezing out all the juices from the vegetables. If you find it's not strong enough, then just boil to reduce for 10 minutes. Check the seasoning and store in the refrigerator for 2 to 3 days.

Chicken Stock
Makes approx. 2.5 litres

2 chicken carcasses, chopped • 500 g chicken wings • 4 litres water
• 2 onions, chopped • 2 carrots, diced • 2 celery sticks, sliced • 1 bouquet garni

1. Place the chicken carcasses and wings in a large saucepan. Cover with the cold water and bring to the boil, skimming all the time.
2. Add the vegetables and simmer for 1 hour, partially covered.
3. Strain the clear stock through a fine sieve.

4. When cold remove all traces of fat which will have solidified on the surface. Store in the fridge for no more than 4 days.

Tomato Coulis
4 to 6 servings

450 g tomatoes, peeled, de-seeded and chopped • pinch of sugar
1 clove garlic, chopped • 1 tbsp tomato purée • 80 ml olive oil
1 shallot, finely chopped • chopped herbs
(basil, tarragon, oregano or chevril)

Heat the olive oil in a pan and sweat the shallots and garlic for few minutes. Add the chopped tomatoes and the herbs. Cook gently on a very low heat for about 40 minutes until the sauce has become a thicker, almost lumpy texture. You can use as it is or blend for a smooth texture.

Chef's tip: This coulis can be used as an excellent vinaigrette if added to balsamic vinegar and olive oil.

Basic Vinaigrette
Makes 220 ml

30 ml olive oil • 120 ml sunflower oil • 40 ml white wine vinegar
• 1 tsp of sugar • 1 tsp Dijon mustard • salt and pepper • 2 tbsps water

Place the salt, pepper, mustard and vinegar in a bowl and stir with a whisk. Add the oils slowly and whisk together until they emulsify and are thoroughly combined. Store in a suitable container for later use.

Ratatouille
6 to 8 servings

80 g onions, diced • 100 g courgettes, diced • 100 g aubergines, diced
• 60 g red peppers, diced • 60 g yellow peppers, diced • 2 cloves garlic
• 120 g tomatoes, de-seeded, skinned and chopped
• 10 basil leaves, chopped • 120 ml olive oil
• 60 ml tomato sauce (see p 91) • salt and pepper

1. Heat 80 ml oil in a large saucepan and begin by cooking the aubergine and courgette for approx. 5 minutes each. Remove and place on a paper towel to absorb excess oil.

2. Heat the remaining oil, add the onion, diced peppers and cook for a few minutes. Add the garlic, the chopped tomatoes, tomato sauce, the aubergines and the courgettes. Mix together gently, and simmer for 10 minutes or until the vegetables are tender but not too soft as they should retain some shape.

Cocktail Sauce · 4 servings

6 to 8 tbsps mayonnaise (see below) • 1 tsp Worcestershire sauce
• 4 drops tabasco sauce • 1 tsp lime or lemon juice
• 2 tbsps tomato ketchup • 1 tbsp brandy [optional] • salt

Add all the ingredients to the mayonnaise. Stir and taste to check the seasoning.

Pesto · 4 to 6 servings

3 tbsps chopped basil • 1 tbsp chopped flat leaf parsley • 60 g pine nuts
• 2 cloves garlic • 45 g Parmesan cheese • 180 ml olive oil,
seasoning to taste

1. Place all the ingredients in a food processor and mix until smooth.
2. Transfer the mixture to a bowl and cover with clingfilm.
3. Refrigerate until required.

Mayonnaise · 6 to 8 servings

2 egg yolks • 1 tbsp mustard • 1 tbsp white wine vinegar
1 tbsp lemon juice • 260 ml sunflower oil • salt and white pepper

1. Put the egg yolks, mustard, vinegar, and seasoning in a bowl and mix together thoroughly, preferably using a wire whisk.

2. Add the oil in drops at first, whisking constantly. Then, when the mayonnaise begins to thicken, add slightly larger amounts, but continue whisking until all the oil has been added, and the sauce has become thick and smooth.

3. Add the remaining lemon juice and mix thoroughly.
4. For a thin mayonnaise, water down with a little warm water or cream.
5. Store in the refrigerator covered for 10 days.

Butter Sauce or Beurre Blanc   *4 servings*

1 shallot, finely chopped • 60 ml white wine vinegar
• 120 ml dry white wine • 80 ml whipping cream • 140 g unsalted butter, diced
• 2 tbsps water • a dash of lemon juice

1. Place the chopped shallot, vinegar and wine in a saucepan. Bring to the boil and reduce to about 3 tbsps.
2. Add the cream and reduce a little more.
3. Over a very low heat, whisk in the diced butter until amalgamated. If the sauce is too thick add 2 tbsps water, then pass through a fine sieve.
4. Add the dash of lemon and season to taste.

Chef's tip: This sharp buttery sauce can be used for a number of fish dishes and can be varied by adding chopped tomatoes, mustard, finely chopped vegetables, single or mixed herbs.

White Wine Cream Sauce   *4 to 6 servings*

180 ml white wine • 2 shallots, finely chopped • 80 g butter
250 ml fish stock (see p 86) • 160 ml whipping cream • salt and pepper

1. Cook the shallots gently with 40 g butter until transparent.
2. Add the wine and reduce by three quarters.
3. Add the fish stock, bring to the boil and reduce further to three quarters.
4. Now, add the cream and simmer for 3 to 4 minutes, then pass through a fine sieve.
5. Whisk the rest of the butter into the sauce before serving.

Fresh Pasta
Makes approx. 450 g

300 g plain white flour • 1 egg + 2 egg yolks
• 1 tbsp olive oil • 30 ml water • a pinch of salt

1. Place all the ingredients in a food processor and mix briefly until the dough has come together.
2. Remove from the machine and knead the dough lightly on a floured surface for approx. 2 minutes until smooth and elastic. If it is sticky, add a little extra flour.
3. Wrap with clingfilm and leave to rest for 1 hour before use.

Chef's tip: A pasta machine is the easiest method of rolling out the dough. Alternatively, use a rolling pin.

Dark Sauce
Makes approx. 1 litre

1.5 kg beef bone and veal trimmings • 500 g chicken carcass
• 2 medium onions, chopped • 2 carrots, chopped • 2 celery sticks, chopped • 2 tomatoes • 1 leek, chopped • 100 g mushroom trimmings
• 80 g bacon trimmings • 3 tbsps tomato purée
• 2 cloves garlic • 1 bouquet garni (thyme, bay leaf, parsley sprigs)
• 5 litres water • 1 litre red wine • 120 ml oil

1. Pre-heat the oven to 400°F/200°C/Gas Mark 6.
2. Roast the bones and trimmings with half the oil for 30 to 40 minutes until well coloured.
3. In a separate large stock pot, cook the onion, carrot, garlic, and remaining oil until golden brown.
4. Add the mushrooms and tomato purée and cook gently until brown.
5. When ready, add the bones, trimmings, red wine, bouquet garni, leek and the water to the pot, bring to the boil, skim off any impurities and simmer for 3 to 4 hours.
6. When ready, drain into a saucepan and continue cooking until it is reduced by half.
7. Adjust the seasoning then pass through a fine sieve.
8. Cool and refrigerate. The following day, remove any traces of fat from the surface.

Chef's tip: This basic recipe can be used to give the correct consistency and flavour to the fish and meat recipes.

Tomato Sauce

**450 g ripe tomatoes peeled, de-seeded and chopped • 1 large carrot, chopped
• 1 large onion, chopped • 1 clove garlic, crushed • 20 ml olive oil • 40 g celery, diced
• 30 g tomato purée • 200 ml chicken stock reduced by half (see p 86) • 120 ml dry white wine
• salt and pepper • fresh herbs (parsley, basil, marjoram)**

1. Cook the onion, carrot and celery with the garlic and herbs in oil for a few minutes until softened.

2. Add the tomatoes with the tomato purée, chicken stock and white wine, bring to the boil, and simmer 20 to 25 minutes with the lid on.

3. The sauce can be used as it is or if preferred, liquidise the sauce and push through a fine sieve to give it a smooth consistency. Season to taste.

Chef's tip: To peel the tomatoes, immerse in a bowl of boiling water for 10 to 15 seconds, then plunge into cold water. Tinned tomatoes can be used, especially Italian ones which have a good colour and flavour.

Bechamel Sauce

Makes 300 ml

**300 ml milk • 25 g butter • 15 g plain flour • 1 bay leaf
• 2 slices of onion • 8 black peppercorns**

1. Pour the milk into a saucepan. Add the onion, bay leaf and peppercorns. Bring to the boil then remove from heat and infuse for 15 minutes.

2. Meanwhile, melt the butter in a saucepan. Stir in the flour and cook, stirring for 1 minute.

3. Remove from the heat and gradually pour on the warm milk through a sieve, whisking constantly. Season.

4. Return the pan to the heat and bring to boil, whisking all the time until the sauce thickens and smooth. Simmer for a few minutes.

5. Once cooled, store in a container and refrigerate for up to 3 to 4 days.

Pistachio Herb Crust

60 g brioche breadcrumbs • 40 g flat-leaf parsley
• 20 g curly-leaf parsley • 30 basil leaves • 1 tsps marjoram, chopped
• 120 g softened butter • 1 clove garlic • 80 g pistachio nuts • salt and pepper

1. Place all the ingredients except the breadcrumbs and butter in a food processor and mix until well chopped.
2. Add the butter and continue blending for one minute.
3. Transfer into a bowl and add the breadcrumbs and mix well. Season with salt and pepper.
4. Store in the refrigerator, covered.

Chicken Mousse

240 g chicken breast, skinless • 3 egg white, small • 180 ml whipping cream
• a pinch of cayenne pepper • salt

1. Cut the chilled chicken breast into cubes.
2. Place in a food processor with the egg white, cayenne and salt.
3. Process to smooth paste and add the cream slowly until blended but do not over process.
4. You should end up with a mousse-like texture. If preferred, push through a fine sieve for a smoother mousse.

Red Wine Sauce

300 ml red wine • 3 shallots, finely chopped
• 1 carrot, finely chopped • 1 clove garlic, crushed • 250 ml dark sauce (see p 90)
• 1 tbsp brandy • black pepper • 80 g diced butter

1. Cook the shallots, the chopped carrot and garlic gently with 25 g butter for 2 to 3 minutes until transparent. Pour the red wine and brandy into the frying pan and boil to reduce until almost dry.

2. Add the dark sauce and bring to simmer gently for 10 minutes until coating consistency is reached.

3. Pass the sauce through muslin or a fine sieve, adjust the seasoning, whisk the rest of the butter into the sauce.

Tapenade
6 to 8 servings

220 g pitted black olives • 20 g anchovy fillets • 2 cloves garlic • 15 capers, well drained • 100 ml olive oil • 1 tbsp chopped basil • black pepper

1. Put all the ingredients into a blender.
2. Mix until it has reduced to a paste, approx. 5 minutes.
3. Scrape the mixture into a small jar with a screw-on lid.
4. The tapenade will keep for up to 2 months in the fridge.

Pastry Trellis
4 servings

140 ml water • 115 g plain flour • 70 g butter • 3 to 4 eggs

1. Pre-heat the oven to 360 °F/195 °C/Gas Mark 4.
2. Sieve the flour on to a square of greaseproof paper.
3. Put the water and butter into a saucepan. Slowly bring to the boil.
4. Tip the flour at once into the hot liquid and beat thoroughly with a wooden spoon over the heat until it leaves the sides of the pan.
5. Remove from the heat and leave to cool for a few minutes.
6. Transfer to a mixing bowl and beat the eggs, a little at a time and adding just enough to give a dropping consistency.
7. Grease the outside of a large cup and place upside down on a baking sheet. Spoon the pastry mixture into a piping bag fitted with a fine plain nozzle. Pipe a trellis design over the cup.
8. Bake in the oven for 10 minutes. When cooled, carefully remove the trellis from the cup and store in an airtight container.

Sweet Pastry

300 g plain flour • 200 g unsalted butter • 100 g icing sugar
• 1 egg +1 egg yolk, beaten together • zest of 1 lemon

1. In a bowl cream the butter and icing sugar together until pale and fluffy.
2. Add the eggs and lemon zest and beat to a smooth paste.
3. Fold in the flour and mix until the pastry comes together.
4. Form into a ball and wrap in clingfilm.
5. Place in the refrigerator for 2 hours before use.

Chef's tip: For quicker results an electric mixer can be used.

Filo Pastry Cases

4 servings

8 sheets from ready-made filo pastry
• 30 g melted butter • 1 tbsp dried breadcrumbs

1. Pre-heat the oven to 400°F/200°C/Gas Mark 6. Brush 4 crème caramel moulds on the outsides with butter and 4 moulds on the insides.
2. Lay out filo pastry on a flat surface and cut out 12 circles of 13-14cm diameter using a plate or basin as a guide.
3. Gently and evenly brush a coating of butter over each circle and sprinkle each one with breadcrumbs.
4. Place one of the crème caramel moulds upside down and lay 3 circles of the pastry on top. Now invert another mould on top of the pastry pushing down gently to shape the pastry around the mould. Repeat 3 more times with the remaining pastry circles.
5. Bake in the oven for 8 to 10 minutes, then remove top mould and further bake until golden brown. Cool on a wire tray and remove the inner mould. Cool the cases and store in an airtight container until needed.

Crème Anglaise

6 servings

480 ml milk • 6 egg yolks • 115 g caster sugar • seeds of 1 vanilla pod

1. Gently heat the milk together with the vanilla seeds in a saucepan.
2. Whisk the egg yolks and sugar until light in colour in a separate bowl.
3. Pour the milk into the egg yolks in the bowl, stirring well, then return to the milk pan.
4. Cook very slowly over a gentle heat, stirring constantly, until the mixture thickens enough to coat the back of the spoon. Do not boil the sauce.
5. Remove from the heat and pass through a sieve. Leave to cool. Cover with clingfilm.

Fruit Coulis

4 servings

50 g granulated sugar • 120 ml water • lemon juice to taste
• fresh or frozen fruit: mango, peach, strawberry, peeled and chopped

1. Dissolve the sugar in the water and bring to the boil, until it thickens to a syrup consistency. Cool and set aside.
2. Liquidise the prepared fruit in a blender to a pulped purée.
3. With the blender switched on low, gradually add the syrup, a little at a time, until the whole mixture becomes smooth.
4. Pour the coulis through a fine sieve and refrigerate or use as desired. The purée also freezes well.

Chef's tip: While fruit is equally good fresh or frozen, if using frozen fruit be careful to add less of the sugar syrup to the purée, since the water content of the fruit will have become greater after freezing.

The Author

Born in the picturesque village of Valentine, France, Chef François discovered at an early age the pleasure of French cuisine. After completing an apprenticeship in his home country, his talents soon led him around the world via Barbados and England, where he opened his own highly acclaimed restaurant 'Le Provençal'.

François first arrived in the Gulf in 1983. He is well known for the distinctive taste of the dishes he prepares daily for 'Le Classique' restaurant, at the exclusive Emirates Golf Club. His cuisine has naturally developed to reflect the influence of the Orient and the abundance of spices and other products from the East and the Mediterranean, all available in the Gulf markets.

EMIRATES GOLF CLUB DUBAI

Acknowledgements

Iam very grateful to the following people who have contributed so much to this book; Moira Leitch who gave me the idea for the book in the first place; Colin Leitch who made the sponsorship possible and Carole Read for all her help and encouragement. At Motivate Publishing I would like to thank Catherine Demangeot for persuading me it was possible; Kate John for editing the book and from whom I received invaluable support and guidance and Adiseshan Shankar, who photographed my recipes so artistically and who will be a friend forever. I would particularly like to mention Andrew Millar who believed in me and brought me back to Dubai, for which I will always be grateful – and my wife Patricia, who has always encouraged me and has supported me throughout my career as a chef over the past 27 years. Finally, thanks to

 Al-Futtaim motors **TOYOTA**

whose support made possible the publication of this book.